THE
Archive Photographs
SERIES

CHISLEHURST
TO
SIDCUP

Chisleburst.

Looking down Red Hill towards Chislehurst from beside the White Horse, now the Penny Farthing, during the winter of 1910. The houses on the right have been demolished to make way for the Library and Sainsbury's. Left is the Church of the Annunciation before its tower was built. The postcard was sent to Bombadier W.G. Cooling, of the 187th Brigade, R.F.A., stationed at Leipje Barracks, Eushott, Hants, by his eldest sister, Flo.

THE
Archive Photographs
SERIES

CHISLEHURST
TO
SIDCUP

Compiled by
Hilary Heffernan

CHALFORD

First published 1997
Copyright © Hilary Heffernan, 1997

The Chalford Publishing Company
St Mary's Mill, Chalford,
Stroud, Gloucestershire, GL6 8NX

ISBN 0 7524 0778 3

Typesetting and origination by
The Chalford Publishing Company
Printed in Great Britain by
Bailey Print, Dursley, Gloucestershire

Dedicated to Madeleine and Mauro
with love
on the occasion of their wedding.

Chislehurst Pond from the top of Chislehurst High Street in Summer, with Lash's Forge on the left where Barclay's Bank is now. After the end of the Second World War, Lash's still made wooden cartwheels. Michael Cooling remembers the wooden shutters on their windows being rubbed down and painted about fifteen times over the Summer, achieving a high gloss finish. As horse transport gave way to motor cars, Lash's adapted to the times and maintained vehicles as well as horses. One of their customers was the Bilbrough family.

Contents

Acknowledgements

My grateful thanks go to the following contributors who have allowed free access to their premises, significant collections of photographs and documents: Dr Andrew Bamji (Director of Medical Education, QMH); James J. McGrane of A. Bilbrough & Co. Ltd London; Mrs Pearl Bull; Pam and David Dyer of Frognal Manor Equestrian Centre; Nigel Pearson and Maureen Finlay of Chislehurst Golf Club; Michael Cooling of Cooling's Nurseries Ltd, Knockholt; Derek Lamb of Lamb Associates Publishing Consultants; Val Walter rtd Headmistress of Babington House School; Terry Moyle, Head of Geography at Coopers School; Margaret Tripp of Farringtons School; Roy and Audrey Grant of Vale Mascal; Thelma, John and Valerie Jenkins of Camden Ridge; Doris Keane, Guide Captain of Orpington and Barbara Waine of Cheltenham.

I would also like to thank Bruce Hurn of the Chislehurst History Society; Margaret Crawley of Chislehurst Antiques; PC Connell and colleagues of Chislehurst Police Station; Father Patrick Michael O'Leary of St. Mary's Catholic Church; Revd John Allen, Jean and Duncan James and Valerie Watkins, all of St. Nicholas's Parish Church; Revd Michael Adams of Christ Church; William (Father Bill) and Mrs Beer of the Church of the Annunciation; Revd Jim Pennington and Olive Greenway (Jnr Church Co-ordinator) of the Methodist Church; Dr Griffin of Chislehurst Golf Club; Mrs D. Hayward for lending old maps of the area; Mrs Brenda Dignam and daughter; Dr G. Miller for *Snowdrift on Chislehurst Common*; J.R. Beatty of Foreman & Beatty diamond mounters, for their pictures of The Bull's Head and The Queen's Head; Jonathan de Maid of JDM Estate Agents; Jean and Michael Crossfield of The Kent Hounds, Chelsfield; Head Librarian Roy Hopper of Chislehurst Library; Diane Rimmer of Goldsmith's College; Mrs F. Draper of Chislehurst; Mrs Perfect, landlady of The Bull in Royal Parade; Bill and Stuart Davies, Secretary and Captain of the Chislehurst Cricket Club; Mr and Mrs Lloyd of Place Cottage; Richard Gabriel Heffernan for his support and interest; Steve 'Jonky' Hart for information on Smokey Joe and to Guy Osborn, Rattens, *Antique and Craft Mews*, whose numerous and welcome coffees and cakes sustained me during my Chislehurst Quest.

Finally, my thanks and apologies go to anyone whose material or assistance has helped towards the publication of this book but whom I have inadvertently failed to acknowledge by name.

Introduction

In ancient Britain, when settlements were few and far between and a well situated cave was considered a luxurious residence, a wandering group looking for an update on their old home discovered an area of gravelly woodland with a plentiful supply of good water. The wanderers found the soft chalk easy to scrape into cave-sized holes using simple tools made from handy flintstones and Chislehurst was under way. The Anglo-Saxon chisel, chisle, or coesil, indicated gravel or pebbles, while hurst meant woodland, and so Chislehurst (or Cheseladam/ Chiseludam/Chiselwood) came into being.

From such modest beginnings Chislehurst continued as a desirable area to the present day. Although Crown land, the village was not included in the Domesday survey, even though Eltham, St Paul's Cray and Orpington are noted. The twelfth-century church mentioned in two Anglo-Saxon charters was part of a gift by Henry II to the Rochester monks. By the mid-thirteenth century, Scadbury Manor and Frognal were built, as was a small settlement along Perry Street. During London's seventeenth-century plagues, those able to afford it left the city. Many came to Chislehurst, settling mainly around Perry Street. The High Street was not established until the early nineteenth century.

This still relatively small north-west Kent village has been home to English nobility, France's Imperial Family and the famous (and infamous), glad to escape the city bustle and ills, being a mere thirteen miles from London should their presence be required. The estate owners, as social equals, were on visiting terms and regularly held lavish entertainments in their homes. Royalty and courtiers frequently attended social functions at the numerous fine residences, many of which survive. John de Scathebury, Sir Francis Walsingham, Sir Richard Betteson and Lord Sydney all owned Scadbury at one time. Lord Castlereagh lived at Loring Hall, North Cray Road; William Camden at Camden House; Baron Hotham at Coopers; Sir John Boyd, Bt. lived at Danson Hill; Sir Philip Warwick and the Sydneys at Frognal House; Sir Richard Calvert resided at Hall Place; Sir Francis Burdett at Vale Mascal and Sir John Tash built Mount Mascal, which was successively owned by Sir John Leman, Sir Robert Ladbroke, Sir William Calvert, Sir John Fitch-Barker and The Hon. George Richard Savage Nassau. Col. North built Avery Hill and William Morris built The Red House. Other large houses in the area still in situ at this time were Foxbury, Farringtons, Sidcup Place and Elmstead Grange (now Babington House School). Several retired Lord Mayors of London took up residency in the village. It became the last home of ex-Emperor Napoleon III, his family and retinue when exiled from France and the illegitimate daughter of Irishman Charles Stewart Parnell's wife, Kitty o'Shea, a famed beauty, is buried in St Mary's churchyard. There were seven millionaires in Chislehurst before the First World War. Webb's *History of Chislehurst* notes that gentle families living here in the fifteenth century were Cheeseman, Cavell, Ellis, Dynely, Comport, Manning, Miles, Dene, Colman, Welshe, Neweman and Shott. By the mid-sixteenth century, around sixty persons were domiciled in the village. At the beginning of the nineteenth century, 1207 residents were recorded, increasing to over 5000 by the end of the century.

Despite modern housing estates, Chislehurst is still surrounded by large tracts of wooded common land and some are the remains of former large estates within the area of St Paul's Cray, St Mary's Cray, Keston (as far as Bromley), Orpington, Eltham, Bexley and Sidcup.

The village, however, has not escaped its share of villainy: in the nineteenth century, two dastardly double murders hit the broadsheet headlines; the police had been called to the case from London and Maidstone as there was only a small local police station at the time.

The nineteenth-century village school of St Nicholas is opposite the church. The locality is fortunate to be served by several well-established, quality schools, some of which contributed to this book.

Chislehurst remains in two parts split by the Common, ensuring the High Street and Royal Parade maintain a semblance of rurality with two nearby wooded ponds enjoyed by humans and wildfowl alike. Sadly, few of the original businesses have survived in the area: although many old shop premises remain, most have changed their field of trade. The villagers are, however, well catered for with teashops, restaurants and interesting pubs. There is still a saddlers and cornstores at Frogpool Manor Equestrian Centre on Perry Street.

Long before the advent of the railway, horses were a local feature. Several riding stables and schools are in the area, enjoying the somewhat restricted use of local wooded bridle paths, farmland and country lanes while being within hacking distance of more open country. The extensive commonlands are protected by the Chislehurst Commons Conservators who ensure the continuation and preservation of these ancient public lands and rights of way.

Michael Cooling recollects that Chislehurst's first buses were single-deckers. Passengers had to dismount at the bottom of Chislehurst, Station Hill, walk up the steep slope and remount at the top. Before the First World War, the Station yard was crammed with carriages waiting to take the gentry back to their estates from the City: later it was crowded with private cars volunteering to take the wounded to Queen Mary's Hospital.

Above all, Chislehurst is a delightful place; I met the friendliest people in my quest for memorabilia and photographs. Everyone to whom I spoke offered at least one possible source, local anecdote, historic note or one or more of the largely private pictures which have made up this book.

This was the village school from 1869. It is opposite the church and next to the Crown Inn. The village school was previously in the house next door. The present Headmaster is Mr J.P. McDermott. Nearby is The Cockpit, which is said to be ancient and to have had various uses from cock fighting to village meets.

One

Chislehurst Village

Although Chislehurst rambles over a wide area it retains the cohesion and atmosphere of an old village. The police station is Victorian and many of the old houses and shop buildings remain. The streets are shaded by trees while the High Street's Prickend leads immediately to woods and two village ponds. In the opposite direction, White Horse Hill follows on to Mottingham and more modern housing.

The village is blessed with interesting churches, notably St Nicholas's, St Mary's, St Patrick's, Church of the Annunciation, Methodist Church and Christ Church. Unusually, the Parish church of St Nicholas is located some way from the High Street, and is situated in Church Row off Royal Parade. This is because the village originally centred on Perry Street; the High Street was a nineteenth-century development. Nearby is the Church of St Mary's where Napoleon III and the Prince Imperial were buried before being moved to Farnborough, Hants.

Like most villages, Chislehurst has a fittingly dignified war memorial to commemorate those local people who gave their lives in the two wars. As well, a large but simple cross honours the memory of Louis, Prince Imperial, Napoleon III's only son who fought and was killed in the British Army in Zululand. His body was brought back to Chislehurst. A third notable memorial is to William Willett, inventor of daylight saving; a mixed blessing to most. A unique village sign was carved to commemorate H.M. the Queen's Coronation in 1953 and depicts Thomas Walsingham of Scadbury being knighted by Queen Elizabeth I.

Well before the nineteenth century, Chislehurst was a near-self-sufficient microcosm with its own bakery, market gardens, locally ground flour, farms, saddlers, laundry and blacksmith's forge. By social division the population was partitioned roughly into three types: the prosperous elite, whose wealth kept in work and provided a living for those labouring and living on their estates, and the merchants, shopkeepers and others who not only supplied essentials for the labourers but also for the large houses who benefitted the village with their imported wealth.

The centre of Chislehurst's law and order, the Victorian police station, celebrated its centenary in 1993 with PC Peter 'Barney' Connell and colleagues. The station had not been built when the Bonars were murdered at nearby Camden Place. Hay is still placed in the hay rack beside the door and the familiar blue lamp does its faithful duty.

The Water Tower was an interesting building beside Chislehurst Common until 1963 when it was demolished. Barbara Waine lived near the Tower, with its internal spiral staircase, and recalls the road narrowed sharply where it went through the archway. This caused many accidents and victims were sometimes taken to Bank House to wait for the doctor.

Attached to Farrington's estate were these 'tied' cottages on Perry Street. Servants lived in, either in attic rooms at the house or in purpose-built tied-to-the-job housing for families working on the estate. Usually if a servant lost their job they lost their accommodation, too. The cottages were later used as classrooms.

Workers were well accommodated at Farringtons, as these Malthouse cottages seen across the meadow show. They were demolished in 1931.

Farringtons, Chislehurst. Malthouse Cottages.

A delightful watercolour of 'Snowdrift on Chislehurst Common' on painted 25 January 1881 by George Buchanan Wollaston, (1814-1899), and contributed by Dr Miller.

A WOODLAND WALK

Strolling through St Paul's Cray Common woods. Cissie wrote in 1909: 'Chislehurst Flower Show, it was very good indeed, also Fire Brigade Comp' 7oaks. I am looking forward to the 7th when we hope to go for our holidays, we are going to Margate after all.' In 1925 the Common0 was a wild but pleasant place for a walk.

CHISLEHURST COMMON

The Ponds have always been favourite places for leisure. Rush Pond is an overflow for the main Prickend Pond where, at the turn of the century, a man drives by in his dogcart while two ladies watch their children playing by the water. More` recently, a mother and son feed the geese and gulls at Prickend. The ponds are thought to be old gravel pit workings; the purlieu of early owners of Scadbury.

In 1952 Mr Harold Monk was manager of Martin's Bank, Eltham, having moved there with his wife, Constance and daughter Barbara from Forby, Lancs, before moving to Chislehurst in 1934. He had served in the Forces in the 1914-18 war, first with the 7th King's Liverpool and later the R.F.C. Mr Monk was an Air Raid Warden, on the management committee of Chislehurst C. of E. School, a member of Camden Place Lodge Freemasons, Chislehurst Caves Committee and Chislehurst Cricket Club. He was presented with a gold watch on retirement after eighteen years managing Martin's Bank, Chislehurst.

Outside Bank House stood the Martin's Bank gilt grasshopper sign. Regretfully, this was later stolen. The old gaslight hangs from the wall and a 227 bus passes by. Behind Bank House was the Water Tower where Mrs Clarke lived near her son and his wife.

Barbara Waine, née Monk, lived at
Bank House before the First World War
and is seen here in the garden. During
the war she went to Chislehurst and
Sidcup County Grammar School where
wartime lessons were held in dank
underground shelters during air raids.

Barbara, her mother, Mrs Constance Alice Monk, and father enjoying tea in the garden of Bank
House with an elderly friend.

NOV. 5th 1910. AT WEST CHISLEHURST.

Guy Fawkes Night, Chislehurst Common, photographed in 1910 by Michael Cooling's uncle. Firewood was collected for weeks before 5 November. A 'guy' representing Guy Fawkes, dressed in old clothes stuffed with straw, was hauled atop the bonfire. Village families brought potatoes to roast in the hot embers. Pocket money was saved for weeks to buy fireworks. Fathers lit the often unpredictable fireworks. A 'fizzer' failing to ignite was a great disappointment. Enterprising children made their own fireworks: school chemistry books in the 1950s gave full instructions: copper sulphate produced blue flames, barium nitrate, green, strontium nitrate, red, and magnesium, white flares. 'Provide a piece of burning coal,' instructs an 1891 chemistry book under the heading 'Silver Fire', 'sprinkle upon it a pinch of nitrate of silver. Most lustrous sparks will be immediately thrown out and the surface of the charcoal will be coated with silver' and 'take a crystal or two of Nitrate of Copper, bruise them, then moisten with water, roll up quickly in a piece of lead-foil. Soon the lead-foil will begin to smoke, then take fire and explode with a noise.' Unsurprisingly, such chemicals are now unavailable through the family chemists as one disappointed young lad I know found when he trotted along hopefully with the same chemistry book..

The Bull Inn, Royal Parade, Chislehurst, looking towards the Common and The Queens Head at the top of the High Street. Although these pictures were taken in the early 1900s both pubs still offer a warm welcome. Foreman and Beatty, the diamond cutters, are nearby.

Kemnal Road, Chislehurst.

Gone are the days when automobiles could safely drive down the middle of Kemnal Road as in 1908. A blockhouse, built in the war, is still there today. Few Chislehurst thatched cottages remain. Picture postcards precursed the telephone and were avidly collected. Writes a young lady on the back of a card to her friend '...one of those fellows...bosses at me and my face went crimson. The surprise don't mention it, he was walking along the Parade all swank...'

CHISLEHURST: SIDCUP ROAD.

Silvertta

CHISLEHURST COMMON

This same crossroads is a lot busier today. It is on the site of what was once a racetrack which stretched from Prickend to Heathfield. The trees have grown taller since this 1913 picture of the Methodist Church, Fox & Hounds and Queen's Head was taken.

Two
Chislehurst Churches

Chislehurst is well served by its fine churches; the oldest being the Parish Church of St Nicholas. Many of the rich and famous ended their days in the village and the tombs of the Walsinghams of Scadbury, The Bonars of Camden Place, Edward and Elizabeth Ellis murdered in Petts Wood by their ex-gamekeeper in October 1880 and the land and water speed record holder, Sir Malcolm Campbell are all within its walls. In 1857 the steeple of St Nicholas caught fire and was later rebuilt 5ft taller.

Napoleon III and his family worshipped at St Mary's Catholic Church. The Emperor died in January 1873 and his funeral was a grand state affair. The procession stretching the length of the Common was attended by Queen Victoria, Prince Albert, many Heads of State and French and foreign nobility. The Emperor's granite tomb was a gift from the Queen. Six years later St Mary's saw a second royal funeral: that of the Prince Imperial. His mother had the Mortuary chapel added to the church specially to house the remains of her late husband and son but these were later moved to Farnborough, Hants. Only a marble slab remains set in the floor of St Mary's to remind onlookers of its former associations. In the churchyard lie the sad remains of Kitty O'Shea and Charles Stewart Parnell's illegitimate daughter, Claude Sophie O'Shea, born 15 February 1882 who 'died at dawn' on 21 April, two months later. The Church of the Annunciation, established in 1853, was built in 1870 and, like St Nicholas's, constructed of Kentish ragstone. Unlike most churches it is not lined up to face East. Instead, it is aligned to face the sunrise, North East, on 25 March, Lady Day, to which the church is dedicated. A painting of the Annunciation decorates the rear wall and a striking mosaic is above the screen. These, Christ Church, celebrating 150 years of worship in 1997, the Methodist Church and St Patrick's Catholic Church are all within easy walk of the village centre.

The eleventh century saw the establishment of Catholicism in Chislehurst, which continued until the Reformation. In a revival of faith, St Mary's Catholic Church was built by Captain Henry Bowden of the Scots Fusilier Guards on land opposite his house, 'Cooper's'. The Captain and family are buried in the churchyard, as are several French dignitaries and Dr West, who founded Gt. Ormond Street children's hospital. The Imperial Family regularly worshipped here during their sojourn in the village. The first incumbent was the Revd Baron Gauci in 1853. The present priest is Father Patrick Michael O'Leary.

St Nicholas is the Parish Church of Chislehurst. Since the late eleventh century there has been a church on the site and it retains a Norman font and bracket. Graceful Scadbury Chapel holds the remains of the Scadbury family. A pen and ink drawing of the chapel by the late Mrs Ethel Bilbrough now hangs in the headmistress's study at Babington House School. Racing driver Sir Malcolm Campbell is buried here.

In St Nicholas's churchyard are the twin tombs of Colonel Lewis, his wife and two daughters. He commanded the Royal Artillery during the great sea attack on Gibraltar in 1782. Nearby are the graves of the Bonars of Camden Place, murdered in their bed by their footman, Philip Nicholson.

Barbara Monk went on the annual outing of the Chislehurst Methodist Youth Club in 1947. Lord Hayter of Farringtons unveiling a family memorial in the 1930s. The school of Farringtons maintains close ties with the church and has its own chapel in the school grounds.

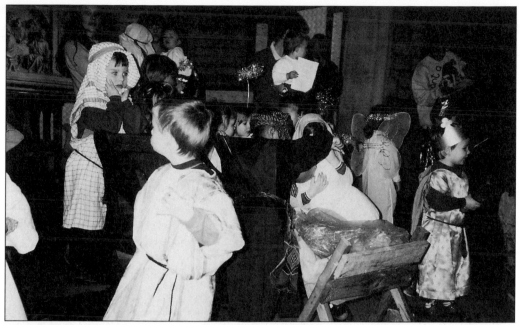

The Chislehurst Mothers and Toddlers Club, started in the mid 1980s, hold a Christmas Nativity play in the church each year when everyone's 'little angels' take part under the benign eye of The Revd Geoffrey Fletcher. The church is 126 years old.

The Methodist newspaper of 1930 offered enlightening books suitable for children's reading.

Christ Church, Lubbock Road, was built on land given by George Wythes of Bickley Park and Nathaniel Strode of nearby Camden Place and celebrated its centenary in 1972. The stipend of the first incumbent, Revd W. Fleming, was partly derived from an Endowment Fund, including generous pew rents at £1.10s. per annum. Babington House School pupils attend services here.

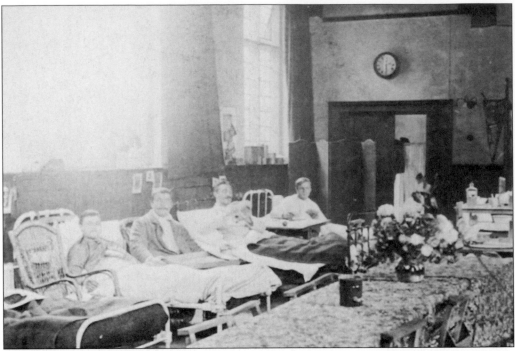

In October, 1914, when wounded soldiers were returned home to Chislehurst, Christ Church Parish Hall was converted into a temporary hospital.

In 1877 a Day School was opened in the church's corrugated iron building in adjoining Mill Place.

The Church of the Annunciation in the High Street, Chislehurst, took two years to build and was completed in 1870. It has an impressive interior with fine carvings, stained-glass windows and mosaic. Father 'Bill' Beer is particularly proud of the 8 bells made by Taylor's of Loughborough. The church has no spire, money being short at the time, so the separate bell tower was built later. Because of this there was no need for windows at the top of the main church tower, which were bricked up.

The congregation of St Patrick's have a most unusual church. In these days when churches are deserted and turned into theatres, housing and craft halls, St Patrick's is the village cinema 'flea-pit' converted into a church. Mrs Barbara Waine stands outside. Lucky parishioners sit in the original tip-up cinema seats and the projection box has been turned into a balcony.

Three
Frogpool Manor

On Perry Street, once a quiet country lane and now a busy major road, is Frogpool Manor Equestrian Centre. Formerly Butt's Farm and later Frogpool Farm, it is one of the largest equestrian retail centres in the U.K. and a focal point for the training of both horses and riders for dressage as well as a livery stable. The old house has been there since the seventeenth century. Carrying on its early farming tradition, Frogpool continues selling livestock feed but it is also a centre for saddlery, riding clothes and equipment. The farm was bought by Pamela Dyer's father, but it was not until Pam and husband David took over, converting the farm to cater for riders and horses, that any real work was done to improve the property. A ditch-cum-small stream running across one field was filled with farm rubbish. This was cleared and converted into a small riding arena for schooling and grazing. All fencing was in desperate need of repair. The existing stabling was renovated and extended to provide more loose boxes and the barn was refurbished. A small barn was converted to a Club Tearoom for clients, adding to the amenities. Although Chislehurst is blessed with many woods and estates there are restrictions on where riders may take their horses. One of the delights of horse-riding is the freedom to roam and this is severely curtailed when only a few bridlepaths are available and horses have to walk along and across busy roads. Fortunately Frogpool's five acres provide three separate areas where riders and horses may train and enjoy. After much dedicated work, Frogpool Manor is now a valuable, friendly centre for North West Kent's horse lovers.

Frogpool Manor in the nineteenth century.

The stables suffered from neglect before Pam and David Dyer renovated them. The sale catalogue page advertised Frogpool at the time Pamela's father bought the farm in 1915.

Lot 21.

(Coloured Pink on Plan.)

A Beautiful XVIIth Century Farm House

known as

" FROGPOOL,"

choicely situated in Perry Street, Chislehurst, close to Frognal Corner.

It is of Brick and Stucco with Tiled Roof, and contains:

Porch Entrance, Hall, Dining Room, about 21 ft. 6 ins. by 17 ft., including Bay, Drawing Room, about 19 ft. by 16 ft. 9 ins., small Smoking Room, Kitchen, Scullery, Larder, Cellar and Pantry, Four Bedrooms, Dressing Room, large Attic Room, Bathroom, Lavatory and W.C., Servants' Room.

Outside are Wood Shed, Stabling for Three Horses, Loft over, and Coach-house.

THE GARDENS

are a very delightful feature of this Property and are beautifully laid out with Tennis Lawn, Flower Beds and Borders.

KITCHEN GARDEN AND ORCHARD.

Let upon Lease to A. P. FORD, Esq., for 7 or 14 years (Lessee's option) from Michaelmas, 1911, at a Rental of

Per £100 annum.

LANDLORD'S OUTGOINGS.

Apportioned Tithe Commutation Rent Charge, 15s. 9d. Value 1915 ... 12s. 2d.

SCHEDULE.

No. on 1/2500 Ordnance Map, 1909 Edition.	Description.	Acreage.
	CHISLEHURST PARISH.	
Pt. 118	Frogpool	1·248

Four

Bilbroughs

Arthur Bilbrough, the first of six children born to Anne and Brooks Priestley Bilbrough, was born in Leeds, Yorkshire, at Park House Gildersome, the Bilbrough's family home since the eighteenth century. They were traditionally linked to the nearby village of Bilbrough. Later, they lived in Ireland before Arthur attended New Brighton College, Lancashire, until aged fifteen in 1856. Through his Uncle Lister, Arthur was fortunate to secure a job in the offices of Pilkington Wilson, owners of the White Star mail clippers on the Liverpool to Australia route. For 5 years apprenticeship he received the princely sum of £80. Seven years later, Arthur and Liverpudlian fellow boarder Albert Cook arrived in London. Arthur borrowed £1,000 from Lister, rented an office and founded a shipping business with Henry Trefal Wilson, becoming Wilson Bilbrough when Albert died. Later, Arthur purchased four White Star clipper ships. With business established, Arthur married Agnes Hodgson, a banker's daughter. Albert, born 18 months later was followed by Harold and Kenneth. In 1865 Arthur repaid Lister's £1,000. In 1870, brother James, an insurance broker, joined the family business and by 1871, teamed up with George Smith of Smith Elder, exporters. It was George who first launched Jane Eyre into the literary world; Charlotte Bronte sent him the manuscript of the book under her pseudonym of Currer Bell and he was so taken with her powerful writing style he published it and, later, sister Emily's Wuthering Heights under the name Ellis Bell. Arthur, prosperous shipping merchant, became a director of Barclays Bank. In 1897 Kenneth married Ethel Dixon, moving to Elmstead Grange from Winton in 1904. The couple entered fully into Chislehurst social life: Kenneth became an Eltham College governor, St Nicholas's churchwarden and joined the Faculties Consultative Committee and they entertained regularly, numbering the Archbishop of Canterbury and Sir Arthur Pearson, founder of St Dunstan's, among their friends. Albert, Kenneth's eldest brother, died in 1908 so Arthur and Agnes Bilbrough moved to Camden Court to be near Kenneth and Ethel. The house was demolished twenty years later and Camden Close was built on the former grounds.

The Bilbrough family with guests visiting England for the coronation of King George V.

Kenneth Leslie Bilbrough was the last of the family to live at Elmstead Grange. Kenneth was never seen without a buttonhole, freshly picked from their garden every morning.

The Rt. Revd Harold Bilbrough, Arthur and Agnes' second son, attended Westminster like his brothers, but then joined the church and went on to become Bishop of Dover, then of Newcastle-upon-Tyne. He preached to George V and Queen Mary in 1921, retired to Chislehurst in 1941 and died in 1950 after 60 years in the cloth.

Arthur Bilbrough at the age of 84.

Officers and cadets aboard the Bilbrough clipper, *North Star*, 19 January 1893. The North Star seen off Port Augusta, Australia, after her maiden voyage in 1893.

Ethel Bilbrough reading beside the pedestal in the forecourt of Elmstead Grange. Ethel was an accomplished artist and pianist and wrote several pieces of music for Boosey & Co. The Jacobean-style house's gardens included 22 acres of woodland, some of which still survives, buttressing the present school against the noise of passing traffic.

Once again Ken has been collecting for St Dunstans, and this year he has far surpassed his fine total of last year as will be seen by the account here given. Moreover Queen Alexandra also wrote him a personal letter of thanks, which was extremely nice of her, for its not Every one who can claim the distinction of having received a letter of gratitude from a Queen! and written in her own hand writing, not Even typed, which makes a great difference. There is something so character-isticless about a type-written letter somehow, it has come from a machine instead of a living being —.

ST. DUNSTAN'S HOSTEL FOR BLINDED HEROES.

QUEEN ALEXANDRA'S LETTER TO MR. KENNETH BILBROUGH

Her Majesty Queen Alexandra, as Patroness of St. Dunstan's Hostel for Blinded Soldiers and Sailors, has personally written a letter of thanks to Mr. Kenneth L. Bilbrough, a Member of Lloyd's and an old school-fellow of Sir Arthur Pearson, expressing her very appreciative thanks for his work on behalf of the funds of St. Dunstan's.

The text of the letter, which was in her Majesty's own handwriting, is as follows:

Sandringham,
Sept. 18, 1917

Dear Mr. Bilbrough,

I have just heard from Sir Arthur Pearson of the truly magnificent sum of £60,000 which you have personally collected and have given to him for the present and after-care of our poor blinded soldiers and sailors, in whose behalf I am so deeply interested.

I wish to express to you my heartfelt and grateful thanks for your splendid effort on behalf of these heroes of the war, and I am proud to be the Patroness of St. Dunstan's Home, where they are so tenderly cared for and looked after by Sir Arthur Pearson, and which has now, owing to you, been so magnificently assisted in its great work.

Believe me,

Yours sincerely,
(Signed) ALEXANDRA.

The splendid sum of £67,000 has been raised in the course of two years through Mr. Bilbrough's systematic appeals to individuals and firms in the shipping, insurance, banking and commercial world, the amount in the first year aggregating £15,000.

This year Mr. Bilbrough made a further appeal for the men of St. Dunstan's, which met with a response even more liberal than the very generous one accorded to him before. A noteworthy addition to the present year's list of donors is found in the names of the two Archbishops and 34 of our Bishops, who have readily responded to and personally signed Mr. Bilbrough's appeal. Altogether Mr. Bilbrough has personally collected nearly £57,000 for the benefit of those heroes who have made so tremendous a sacrifice for the cause of their country and their Allies. Furthermore, by arousing the sympathy of influential friends he has been instrumental in securing an additional sum of about £10,000 for the funds, thereby making a total of £67,000 - an achievement upon which he is to be heartily congratulated.

Ethel, a wealthy, well-educated lady of strong opinions, kept a fascinating diary throughout the First World War, recording personal feelings and wartime events. She and Kenneth contributed generously to the war effort, organising many successful fund-raising events. A page from Ethel's wartime diary shows the newscutting of Queen Alexandra's letter. The Queen was Patroness of St Dunstan's. Her original letter was framed and proudly displayed in the Bilbrough's home. When Kenneth died in 1962 the letter went to St Dunstan's, London.

Arthur Bilbrough was married to Agnes who
died at Camden Close in 1922, aged 84.
Ethel's Winton drawing room was filled
with bric-a-brac, pictures and one of
Kenneth's collection of clocks.

Two of Ethel Bilbrough's watercolours, painted while on holiday abroad.

Elmstead Grange was the Bilbrough's home from 1904. The ivy, threatening to swallow the elegant lines of the building, had to be removed when the house became a school in the 1950s as it would have been a fire hazard The octagonal Turret Room offered fine views across Chislehurst.

Ethel Bilbrough and her sister Mary
with their dog 'Nat' enjoy a summer
afternoon in the garden.

The entrance hall in 1909. Under the
Heritage scheme extensive restoration
was carried out when Babington
House School moved in.
Headmistress Valerie Walter held an
'Auction of Promises' to which Prince
Charles donated a magnum of
specially bottled 'Investiture' sherry.
Nearly £6,000 was raised.

Five

Babington House School

Babington House School was established in 1887 in North Park, Eltham, by Madame Rossel, a Belgian lady with a flair for teaching. With his permission, she named the school after Lord Babington Macaulay, whose work she admired. The school was founded to provide a liberal education for Young Ladies and Small Boys' and was run on the lines of a public school. In 1890 Madame sold the school. Subsequent owner-headmistresses were Mrs Kingsford, Miss Hartley (1892), Miss Gill (1906), Miss MacDermott, the Misses Milne, Miss Berry and Miss Perkins (1930) at which time there were 80 pupils. Miss Berry managed the school during the war years and in 1959 they moved to Elmstead Grange. From these early days Babington has grown, although if the Charitable Trust formed in 1958 had its way the school would be no more. It took considerable parent and pupil power to stop the Trust from closing the school that July. This supportive parental loyalty remains today. Babington exudes a purposeful, caring, happy and dedicated atmosphere. The pupils take pride in their school which maintains a high standard of work. As in the time of Madame Rossel, French is taught from an early age and quickly becomes a second language. The school, which encourages gifted children, was administered by Mrs Valerie Walter until Easter 1997. It is now in charge of Mrs Costin.

Children have the advantage of small classes and the unique features of the house design have been well adapted, with a computer room tucked among the airy attic beams and the servants quarters back stairs leading to the administrative rooms, giving the school a warm family ambience.

Babington House School from the air.

Light, airy classrooms with pleasant views of trees and gardens encourage a relaxed atmosphere and easier concentration. The panelled stairwell with heavy carved balustrade gives these girls access to their upstairs classrooms. Above are stained-glass windows filtering rainbows onto the white stonework balconies opposite.

Six

Frognal House

The present Frognal House was built by Philip Warwick in 1670 on the site of the original thirteenth-century house. Marcus Dyngley bequeathed an unusual division of property to his sons in that each was left a different room in the house. Various owners lived there until Philip Tryon bought it from William Watkins and renovated it to his own taste and this is the house standing today. Dr Andrew Bamji, in his history of Queen Mary's Hospital, records that Thomas Townsend of Scadbury purchased the estate cheaply in 1752 after its previous owner had committed suicide and Chancery sold the house to repay his debts. Thomas demolished Scadbury, intending to rebuild it. He then moved into Frognal, but died shortly after. His son Thomas became Baron, later Viscount, Sydney of Chislehurst having distinguished himself as an eighteenth-century politician during Britain's peace talks with America. It was in his honour that Sydney, Australia, was designated. Several local street names record his association with the area. There is a Botany Bay in both Sydney, New South Wales and Chislehurst. Robert Marsham inherited the joint estates of Frognal and Scadbury on the death of his aunt and uncle, taking the name Townshend to continue the family line. Frognal and its 97 acres were put up for auction in 1915 but no-one was interested - not even the property dealers. In 1916 the house came under consideration as a possible treatment centre for casualties of the battlefields of the First World War and became Britain's first plastic surgery unit.

Frognal House showing the Orangery.

The Long Gallery at Frognal House. The lodge and entrance gates of Frognal among shady trees in 1906, most of which have now gone. It was perfectly safe to walk along this unmade road wheeling a perambulator, unless of course some reckless rider cantered unheedingly along the grassy footpath.

Frognal Avenue. Sidcup.

Seven

Queen Mary's Hospital

An extract from Legs-Eleven *by Captain Belford describing the First World War battle at Bullecourt, France:'... As they pushed up the trench they were met by a party of Germans with flammenwerfer (flamethrowers). Hallahan and Kirkwood each threw a bomb, but young Gillard was killed... The German shelling increased in intensity and many of our boys were killed, wounded or buried. Mates spent a lot of time digging out their (friends) after the frightful shell-bursts. Casualties were very heavy.' On the first day of the Battle of the Somme 60,000 men were slaughtered or badly injured. Their image of a hero's hour with bands playing and the pride of the nation sustaining them ended as terrible carnage took its toll. This, they said, was the war to end all wars. Casualties returning to England with horrific facial disfigurements desperately needed specialist medical care. It must be hard to regard oneself as a hero when the mirror reflects a grotesque version of your self image and revulsion shows even on the faces of loved ones. Queen Mary, Sir Heath Harrison and the Joint War Committee funded surgeon Harold Gillies' vision to establish a centre for plastic surgery able to re-build the faces of the disfigured. Queen Mary's Hospital opened on 18 August 1917 with 320 beds based in Frognal house and purpose-built wooden huts. Patients began arriving immediately. The flood increased, with patients including sailors and pilots, and rose to 600. Patients overflowed into large houses around Chislehurst. Christ Church Hall was commandeered. The surgical staff were military. Surgeons came from world wide to learn their techniques. Some victims still required multiple operations. One patient, Mr Jolly of Yorkland Avenue, Welling, died in the 1970s. Mr Jolly lost part of his jaw and upper palate which were both rebuilt at QMH. In the Second World War, the hospital was used for civilian as well as military patients. Several bombs fell destroying nearly half the beds. QMH nearly didn't survive post-war National Health re-organization, but thanks to local MP George Wallace the hospital joined the NHS. The famous Macmillan Nurses originated in QMH. Miss MacMillan was born in Knoll Road, Sidcup. By 1965 the old huts had disappeared, Frognal House was no longer required: a new, well-equipped hospital was opened close by, which still serves well the needs of people in the area.*

Views of Frognal House, the old huts at QMH and an old soldier patiently sitting in Watery Lane beside the hospital.

An aerial view of Frognal military hospital at Sidcup. At Christmas the ward was decorated cheerfully for its soldier patients. The huts were still being used in 1970 when the author's father was a cancer patient there. At that time gipsies camped in nearby fields, grazing their tethered ponies and gathering the freely-growing wild blackberries.

First World War postcards were often quite elaborate in design. These are embroidered with the insignia of the Royal Armoured Medical Corps with its motto of 'faithful in hardship'. One has a small pocket into which a card bearing a message can be slipped.

Pictures from the official archives of QMH, courtesy of Dr Andrew Bamji. The RAMC cared for the wounded, whichever side they were on. The journey to hospital was often a rough one. A soldier sits below the commandeered transport in his dug-out.

Wounded soldiers and sailors start the journey back to 'Blighty' and proper medical care. Sometimes there were long delays between sustaining a severe injury, having emergency field treatment and being seen by an appropriate surgeon.

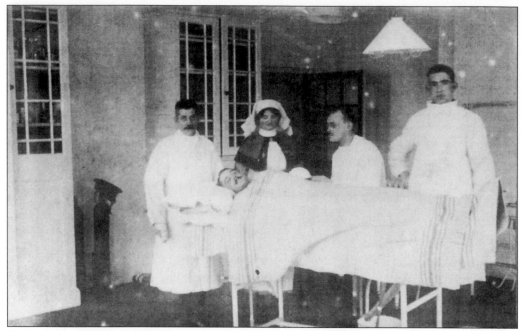

On arrival at 'Queens', or QMH, patients were seen as quickly as possible. The treatment room was simply equipped. The septic ward was kept busy as wounds quickly putrefied. Alexander Fleming did not discover penicillin until ten years after the First World War.

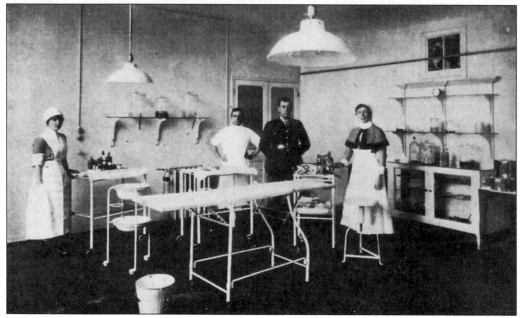

The heart of the original Queen Mary's Hospital was this purpose-built Plastic Theatre with its nursing team.

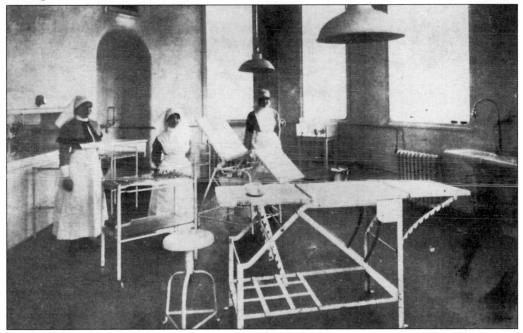

Battle-weary soldiers pose beside their gun. Ironically, Maxim machine guns were manufactured at Crayford, only a few miles from Chislehurst. With so many faces to rebuild, the hospital dental workshop was kept working to maximum capacity.

Two young soldiers in uniform.

With so many patients to feed, the hospital had its own farm and dairy cows. Walking in the tranquil grounds of Frognal must have helped many shell-shocked victims to recover from their ordeal.

Eight

Vale Mascal

Modestly sheltering behind a high wall on North Cray Road is an eighteenth-century gem built by Sir John Tash for his intended marriage to Honoria, daughter of Sir Richard Calvert of nearby Hall Place. The land was owned by The Hon. George Nassau of Mount Mascal, opposite. In 1782, John Madocks bought the house for his eldest son John and wife Frances. John founded the Royal Kentish Bowmen, an archery club patronized by HRH Prince of Wales. In 1794, Sir Francis Burdett MP rented the house, having recently married Sophia, daughter of Thomas Coutts, London Banker. The estate, originally sixteen acres, was partly sold off and now comprises five acres enclosing its own woodland and part of the River Cray. James Lawson, Magistrate, was the next resident. A mysterious admiral lived there at one time and, in memorium of his son killed in battle, built an island mid-river in the shape of a boat, complete with mast and cannons, which can still be seen. The Revd John Egerton and family, then Revd Philip Egerton, who took pride in enhancing the house and grounds, lived here at the turn of the century. More recently, the home was bought by Norman Grant and is now owned by his son Roy Grant and wife Audrey. The period setting is being put to romantic use as Roy and Audrey offer couples the opportunity of holding their wedding in the house and enjoying the ornate gardens, where guests may stroll through the grotto or watch swans and geese sailing along the winding River Cray. The house is decorated in period style, with a butler's dumb-waiter serving food to the panelled dining room, a fine harmonium and parquet floors. At some time the servants quarters in the upper story were replaced with a graceful balustrade and the billiard room became a family annexe, but otherwise the house is little altered from the original.

Fires were a particular hazard in big houses, where a tired servant could be careless in banking up an open fire at night or forget to put a fireguard in front of the smouldering coals. Both Vale Mascal and Mount Mascal suffered fire damage: a few miles away High Elms was entirely razed.

Vale Mascal (variously, Maskal and Mascall) in a tranquil setting. Often geese and ducks adorn the lawn, basking in the sun not far from the River Cray. Nowadays the Grant's dogs, a cashmere goat called Charlie, and Manuel, a friendly llama, all rescued pets, enjoy the grounds.

The Revd P.E. Egerton, a former resident of Mount Mascal in 1902, with his daughter Nell and grandson John. Roy and Audrey's panelled dining room with concealed dumb waiter.

Edwardian and Victorian gardens sometimes incorporated a grotto. Vale Mascal's includes a small cave, fantasy miniature castles and exotic plants. The River Cray winds under several bridges. Sometimes in summer Manuel the llama is allowed to wander free in the woodland.

This eighteenth-century Old Bath House was once part of Vale Mascal property. It boasted an intricate system of sluices, water courses and conduits to feed the walk-in bath.

An 1822 sale poster for the house.

An aerial photograph of North Cray and Old Bexley. Mount Mascal is at the bottom centre of the picture. Vale Mascal and the River Cray are immediately above it across the road. The Old Mill can be seen right of centre in the bend of Bexley Road. The railway runs across the picture. Above it and parallel is Rochester Way with the Tudor Hall Place, top right.

The elegant sitting room looks out onto the lawns and river and is now licensed to hold marriages. The double keyboard harmonium in the dining room.

Nine

Farringtons

Colonel Thomas Farrington married Mary Smith and came to live in Chislehurst at Farrington House, on Perry Street, during the reign of Queen Anne. He died a Major-General in 1712 and his remains are buried in St Nicholas Church, as were those of his descendants. The original house was built in the early seventeenth century for Thomas Blinkhorn and wife Elizabeth, on a 50 acre estate. Lord Sydney removed the fine chestnut panelling in 1822 and the remainder of the contents were put up for public auction. Sadly, the house was abandoned and quickly deteriorated under the acquisitive hands of vandals. In 1832 the estate became part of the dowry of Emily Caroline, Viscountess Sydney, and had various other owners: the Farringtons, Bettensons, Selwyns and Townsends, until 1909 when part of the land was sold to the Girls College Association, later Farringtons Girls School. The school boasted a powerful board of governors, including the Rt. Hon. Lord Hayter Chubb of Chislehurst, of the world-renowned lock and safe company, Revd J. Scott Lidgett, D.D., well known for his benevolence to the poor of Bermondsey, J. Arthur Rank, Esq., D.L., J.P. of film fame, Alderman Sir Charles C. Wakefield, Bt., J.P., Lord Mayor of London, and the Rt. Hon. Sir Kingsley Wood, M.P. The Board was determined the school would be based on Leys public school. 'This great school is rightly regarded as one of the valuable assets of British Methodism, by which the Church provides a first-class education for the daughters of her people' states an article in The Methodist, Sydney, Australia, 12 September 1925. The school remains on the original site but with greatly expanded state of the art facilities. Although having increased in size since those early days, the family atmosphere remains and the girls still benefit from the gracious surroundings and atmosphere.

The Return of Persephone, 30 June 1921. Girls learned the Classics through drama and dance.

Sir George Hayter Chubb, Bart.
128 Queen Victoria Street,
E.C.4.

BUCKINGHAM PALACE

<u>PRIVATE</u>.   3rd May 1926.

Dear Sir George,

      With further reference to the letter which you were kind enough to write to me on April 13th, The Queen now wishes me to let you know that she has given careful consideration to the request that Her Majesty should become Patron of the Farringtons Girls' School.

      I am, however, to say that, before an answer can be given one way or the other, The Queen would naturally desire to know the result of the application for a Royal Charter.

      I hope you will forgive me for not having sent you an earlier reply.

          Believe me, Dear Sir George,
              Yours sincerely,

              Harry Verney.

Sir George Hayter Chubb,
        Bart.
      128 Queen Victoria Street, E.C.4.

The reply from Buckingham Palace to Lord Chubb's suit for Royal patronage of the school.

Miss Davies, Headmistress of
Farringtons. Founders' Day, 1924 saw
the laying of the stone for the
opening of Feren's Hall.

'At the end of June 1924 a very delightful function was celebrated at the great Farringtons School at Chislehurst, when the Queen of England declared the new and beautiful additional buildings opened. It was a perfect day, with royal sunshine, and crowds gathered to witness the great event and catch a glimpse of Queen Mary'. (*The Methodist*, 12 September 1925)

H.M. Queen Mary, the Board of Governors, ladies in waiting and Miss Davies listen to Lord Hayter giving the Governors' Address. Above are two portraits of Lord Haytor.

Portrait of Queen Mary presented to Farrington's by Mr B.H. Granvill, one of the Board of Governors. A programme was specially printed to mark the occasion of H.M. the Queen's visit.

Programme

❦

HER MAJESTY THE QUEEN will arrive at the main entrance of the New Assembly Hall, at 3.30 p.m., and will be received by

The Head Mistress, Miss Alice H. Davies,

The Chairman, Sir George Hayter Chubb, Bt., J.P., and Lady Chubb, and

The Vice Chairman, The Rt. Hon. T. R. Ferens, P.C.,

who will escort HER MAJESTY to the Dais, the National Anthem being played by the String Band of the Royal Artillery.

When THE QUEEN reaches the Dais, the following gifts will be offered to HER MAJESTY:

The Senior Prefect will present a bouquet of roses.

A Fifth Form Girl will present a casket in art needlework containing photographs of the buildings and grounds.

Two Girls of the Junior House will present a programme, and a silver box containing small photographs.

Tea on the Lawn for V.I.P.s and parents, Founder's Day 1917. The School Chapel was built in 1939 to save pupils long walks across the Common to the Methodist Church.

Architect's impression of what Farringtons should have been. Unfortunately, this was too costly. Farringtons from the air in June 1925.

East House was the original school building. In 1921 former pupils Dorothy Pattinson, Dorothy Brewitt, Joyce Shelmordine, Edith Adam, Gertrude Cockerman (and Grace Walker taking the photo) enjoyed a reunion day at the school.

The School: Miss Davies, staff and all the pupils in 1911. By July 1912 the school had grown rapidly.

Cookery Classes were held in the West Gate cottage, 1914, while drawing and science were taught in the Malthouse Cottages. Across the road in Foxbury Mr Tiarks (father of Henrietta Tiarks) allowed the school to use his private swimming pool four days a week. The 1918 'Joint Board' Examinations were as dreaded by examinees as any tests today.

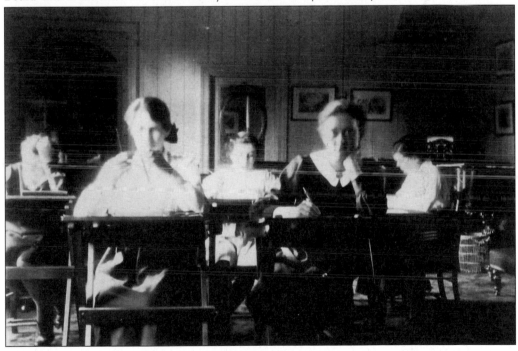

P.E., or Physical Exercise, was a compulsory subject. No matter what the weather, girls dressed in navy knickers (with elasticated legs and a pocket for a handkerchief) and sports shirt. Hoop and vaulting horse displays were all part of Sports Day for parents.

'Precision and timing, girls! Precision and timing!' my gym mistress used to command. These girls have certainly mastered both. Cloche hats were the fashion for the ladies and of course gentlemen wore hats, or how else could they raise them to the ladies?

meeting of the Council was held on
...ay 26th presided over by C. Sutcliffe.

...business before the meeting was:—

...decide who should be head of
...oolroom preparation.

...was decided that in the absence
...Va lower's Form-Captain, the eldest
...mber of Va lower in the schoolroom
...ould be head.

...discuss the question of a school-
...agazine.

...mention several points with regard
...the behaviour of the school.
...Girls must make still more effort to
...eak French on French-days
...Girls must remain in the garden
...until the bell sounds at 3·45.
...All downstairs windows must be

closed at the bottom before supper
and at nine o'clock.
4. Girls must go upstairs for bed
making in an orderly manner
5. No girl must talk when only ju...
inside the door of a room opening
on to the bottom corridor.
6. No girl must sing during her bath
7. Girls must not stay in from Sunda...
—evening Chapel unless they have a
particular reason for so doing ; an...
Girls who do stay in, must employ
themselves quietly.
M.T. Moon. 20/6/24.

Schoolchildren never change. In 1922 the VI form and Form Captains formed a School
Council. In their day book they complained that girls ran down the corridor, were slow replying
to Miss Davies's 'Good Morning' and made too much noise. Two years later they were still
reporting similar problems.

FARRINGTONS GIRLS SCHOOL.

TELEPHONE:
CHISLEHURST 236

FARRINGTONS,
CHISLEHURST.

May 1939.

Dear Sir (or Madam),

Re Evacuation of Farringtons in event of War.

The Governors are officially advised that Chislehurst is in a neutral area, and is not considered as being a danger zone. The Governors have come to the conclusion, however, that the School could be more easily operated in War time if moved to modern Hotel premises attractively situated at Babbacombe, Devonshire, of which the School would have exclusive use.

It is impossible to say definitely whether this could be done, for two reasons, namely, the difficulty of transport, and the possibility of the Hotel at Babbacombe being commandeered.

It would help the Governors in making provisional arrangements if you would be good enough to confirm that you would wish your daughter to go with the School to Babbacombe in the event of War.

I am instructed by the Governors to state that they have not received any Government request or recommendation that the School should be moved, nor have they any reason to consider that War is imminent, or indeed inevitable, but they are merely wishful of taking such precautionary measures as may appear to be advisable.

For this reason they are having shelters prepared at Farringtons under expert advice, and these, of course, will afford some considerable measure of protection in any emergency, pending the ultimate removal, if such proves to be practicable.

Awaiting the favour of your early reply,

I am,
Yours faithfully,

Secretary to the Governors.

Despite this Governors' letter to parents, on 27 August 1939, the school evacuated to the Trecarn Hotel, Babbacombe, Devon. When the R.A.F. commandeered the hotel in 1940, Farringtons returned to Chislehurst.

The School in 1930 and 1933.

Ten
Transports of Delight

Chislehurst's first buses were single-deckers. Passengers had to dismount at the bottom of Chislehurst Station Hill and remount at the top of the hill. This was a wealthy area, with seven millionaires living in the village before the First World War. The railway station yard overflowed with carriages waiting to take the gentry from the City back to their estates. Children sent to collect newspapers newly delivered from London to Chislehurst station frequently hitched clandestine rides sitting on the rear axle of a carriage. Alert passers-by would warn the coachman who flicked his whip to reach underneath the vehicle so any hitch-hiker had to be nippy to dismount or be caught by the stinging lash. Motoring was in its infancy and in 1934 on introduction of the new driving test Kenneth Bilbrough wrote to his friend Revd Oscar Hardman 'You probably know all the enclosed hints, but... There is a general courtesy of the road. This... generally speaking means giving way to the 'road hog'. Please remember that your car is not as powerful as a great many cars and lorries on the road and therefore never try to pass anything when you cannot see at least a 1/4 mile in front of you. After long experience we have always found that if you lie behind a lorry for some little time and do not blow him off the road he will give way and wave you on...You say that you may not drive more than 30 miles an hour. I should think it would be a long time before you could drive at this pace for any length of time with safety to yourself and others. With a car more than three times your horsepower our travelling speed is from 30 to 32 and an average per day of about 25, but this means safety. It is a good thing to keep your petrol tank fairly full and though presumably Lash has looked after your sump, watch your oil gauge...and new oil put in after the next 500 miles. I do not understand your teacher not having explained to you about cleaning your plugs... I clean mine about every 300 miles... In giving hand signals it is a good thing to stretch your right hand out as this gives the fellow behind a proper idea of what you are going to do. Some people make a habit of waggling 2 fingers outside the window, this is swank and very selfish. Happy motoring.'

Kenneth and Ethel Bilbrough outside Elmstead Grange in their Packard, 1920.

The Bilbroughs set off with Ethel's easel packed in the car. Kenneth drove a custom-made Rolls Royce Phantom 111 for his final 22 years with central gear lever, 4-piece wind screen, no mascot, 2 spare wheels, white dials with black figures, a green body and black mudguards. Sold to Dr John Fischer, of Missouri, USA with 34,000 miles on the clock, it had averaged 1,500 miles per annum.

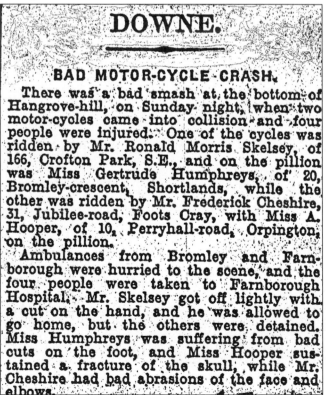

DOWNE.

BAD MOTOR-CYCLE CRASH.

There was a bad smash at the bottom of Hangrove-hill, on Sunday night, when two motor-cycles came into collision and four people were injured. One of the cycles was ridden by Mr. Ronald Morris Skelsey, of 166, Crofton Park, S.E., and on the pillion was Miss Gertrude Humphreys, of 20, Bromley-crescent, Shortlands, while the other was ridden by Mr. Frederick Cheshire, 31, Jubilee-road, Foots Cray, with Miss A. Hooper, of 10, Perryhall-road, Orpington, on the pillion.

Ambulances from Bromley and Farnborough were hurried to the scene, and the four people were taken to Farnborough Hospital. Mr. Skelsey got off lightly with a cut on the hand, and he was allowed to go home, but the others were detained. Miss Humphreys was suffering from bad cuts on the foot, and Miss Hooper sustained a fracture of the skull, while Mr. Cheshire had bad abrasions of the face and elbows.

Despite slower speeds, there were still road accidents in the 1930s.

82

A solid-tyred 1910 automobile at Shepherd's Green Corner, Sidcup Road. Walking past in the late evening with her large covered basket, a woman wears a white apron to keep her long skirt clean.

Barbara Waine's father, Mr Monk, photographed a First World War Zeppelin flying over Chislehurst .

Michael Cooling's picture postcard of Chislehurst's first double-decker bus in front of what is now The Chestnut cafe. The buildings behind comprised a dairy, Peppers sweetshop and a hairdressers. These and the Fox & Hounds were demolished during an air-raid. The pub was rebuilt.

The P.S.A. Cycle Club at 7 a.m. in front of George Cooling's newsagency and stationers, West Chislehurst for a 17 mile Easter Monday ride. Behind the shop was George's photographic studio.

A First World War sergeant with his well-maintained army bicycle.

Four young riders out for a morning hack across the Common.

Barbara Waine's granddad Moore with one of the horses he trained to high step for carriage-driving. Tails of carriage horses were 'docked' to prevent them from catching in the wheels.

One of the first private automobiles on Chislehurst Common was this solid-tyred coach built motor car owned by Uncle Charlie Cooling and family.

Sadly, part of this photograph is missing. Uncle William Cooling and family are out for a ride in their governess' cart on Chislehurst Common. Next to them is Fanny Cooling.

Off to war in a First World War lorry used as a troop carrier. The solid tyres must have given an uncomfortable ride over long distances.

Looking leafier than its modern counterpart, Sidcup Station still with its original gas lamps. The station was built in 1836.

Eleven
The Cooling Family

Grandfather George Cooling, a butler, arrived in Chislehurst in around 1870 from Ripon, worked in his brother William's poultry shop on Royal Parade, then opened his own poultry and fish shop in the High Street. Later, he ran a newsagency, stationers and large, busy photographic studio, employing four full-time staff. George Cooling married Elizabeth and lived at 39 High St. with their seven sons and three daughters. Walter and George were the village photographers. Most photographs of the village taken early in the century were either by Walter, George or one of Cooling's staff. The family knew when grandfather had been taking photographs: his eyebrows would be singed away by magnesium flares. On leaving school Arthur, the sixth child, joined the Post Office, a secure, pensionable post; working 4am to 10pm 6 days a week with time off mid-day. Arthur preferred soil to sorting, using his free time to grow vegetables on rented land, now Belmont Lane, for sale to local greengrocers. During the First World War he was seriously wounded when a German shell exploded in his trench, almost burying Arthur alive. He was the sole survivor. After convalescence he returned to the Post Office, bought Little Farm poultry smallholding behind the High Street, working 14 hour days, often by oil lamp. In 1930 he married Miriam Bentley. They kept chickens, a popular and rewarding pastime. Arthur was secretary of the flourishing Chislehurst Poultry Society whose shows attracted exhibitors from across the UK, even Royalty.

Chislehurst housing increased between the wars; so did the demand for plants. Cooling's thrived, curtailed only by the advent of the Second World War. Tomatoes replaced flowers by Government order. This became an unexpectedly hazardous job when bomb blasts and V1 rockets shattered the greenhouse glass no less than three times. Arthur became an air raid warden. Excessive Government paperwork enforced the closure of the poultry farm.

After the war, the land again grew flowers and Arthur became a Post Office Inspector, retiring honourably in 1954 having worked faithfully for 45 years in a job he disliked. Son Michael did National Service, returning home from Germany in 1955 to join Arthur in the nursery. His youthful radical ideas were not always well received, but selling fresh-cut flowers proved so successful they expanded the business to accommodate this. Arthur regarded the outlay of £37 for such things as fertilizer for their first garden centre in 1960 an imprudent risk. In 1966, partly retired, he died of a heart attack in the nursery he loved. In 1990 the enterprise moved to Knockholt, where Michael and son Paul carry on the business carefully founded and nurtured by Arthur.

Chislehurst Pond in the snow, 1909. Arthur Cooling sits on his sledge with Ernest and Albert, two of his brothers.

Herbert Cooling working in the grape house at Foxbury, Kemnal Road, Chislehurst. A crop of grapes any gardener would be proud of. They enthusiastically entered the competition between head gardeners of local estates as to who could supply the finest, earliest grapes and exotic fruits for their House.

The Chislehurst and Bromley Cooling families gathered together for a picnic on Bromley Common, early 1900s.

Percy Cooling dressed for work at Young and Worger's Poultry and Provisions shop, in the early 1900s.

The Cooling family plant a tree in Royal Parade. Their two delivery carts stand ready. The business next door is an unusual combination of undertaker and decorator.

Arthur Cooling with five brothers and father (George) ploughing their nursery land in Chislehurst.

William Cooling and Mr Wright at the Bromley Common Nursery. The cat looks very comfortable high on his perch.

GEORGE COOLING,
Born November 6th, 1860.

ELIZABETH CATHERINE COOLING,
Born November 24th, 1860.

SONS AND DAUGHTERS
OF
GEORGE & ELIZABETH CATHERINE COOLING,
OF CHISLEHURST.

WALTER GEORGE COOLING	... Born May 28th, 1887
FLORENCE CAROLINE COOLING ...	,, Aug. 19th, 1888
HERBERT COOLING...	,, May 12th, 1890
FRANK COOLING	,, Oct. 14th, 1891
ALICE MAUD COOLING	,, Mar. 17th, 1893
ARTHUR COOLING ...	,, Nov. 9th, 1894
ERNEST COOLING	,, June 17th, 1896
HILDA COOLING	,, Oct. 19th, 1897
ALBERT COOLING ...	,, Dec. 9th, 1899
PERCY EDWARD COOLING ...	,, July 13th, 1901

Arthur Cooling, father of Michael, was the sixth child of George and Elizabeth.

George and Elizabeth's ten children taken about 1906. Frank, Ernest, Walter, Arthur and Herbert on the back row. Percy, Alice, Hilda, Florence (the postcard writer) and Albert.

George Cooling and his sons.

Walter, Florrie, Arthur, Ernie, Hilda, Albert and Percy with their mother. Both pictures were taken in the early 1900s.

George Cooling looking smart in his butler's uniform when at Ripon, aged seventeen. Later, he frequently buttled freelance in the evenings at various large local houses, including Camden Place.

Percy Cooling worked for Young and Worger, provisioners, for a while. This later became Cullens. The windows were illuminated by two large gas lamps at night. The YMCA triangle indicates a nearby hostel, and Salutaris water is advertised.

Cooling's the Photographers took most of the photographs of events in and around Chislehurst in the late nineteenth and first half of the twentieth century. Chislehurst put on a fine welcome-home spread for our soldiers returning home from the trenches on 25 June 1919, nearly seven months after the war was officially over.

Camden Grove children's Street Party, 1944.

WEDDING of REV. S.E.B. SERLE & MISS HOWARD 1.6.20

When Miss Howard married the vicar on the 1 June 1920 at the Church of the Annunciation everyone turned out to wish them well.

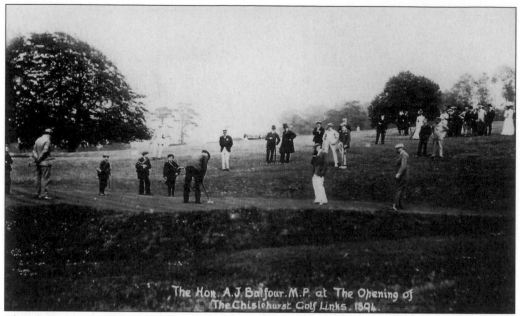

The christening of Chislehurst's newly opened golf club at Camden Park in 1894 by Arthur James, First Earl of Balfour when he was First Lord of the Treasury and Leader of the House.

The Coronation Day parade down Chislehurst High Street on 22 June 1911. The little donkey which won second prize seems reluctant to pass the camera.

A different kind of parade, as the London Regiment march up Chislehurst High Street from Mottingham, past Young & Worger and Chislehurst's garage in 1914.

One of the Chislehurst air guns located on the Common in 1917.

Reserve Battalion of the H.A.C.
at Chislehurst Nov 14th 1914.

By November 1914, Chislehurstians had become quite used to seeing parades marching through the village and were inclined to take them more for granted. As the H.A.C. Reserves march past the Queen's Head round the pond opposite Westminster Bank, only one small boy and a passing carter are there to see them go.

Twelve
Camden Ridge

Off Yester Road in its own cul-de-sac is a unique house designed and built in 1880 by an architect for himself. He built two other houses in the area, one of which was bombed in the First World War. The architect's own home was later bought by Thomas Jenkins who moved to Chislehurst from Cardiff and was proud of his Welsh heritage. Chislehurst seems to have exerted an attraction for enemy aircraft during the war and the Jenkins family were forced to move into a nearby hotel to get away from an UXB which had landed in their garden. However when some time went by without further raids and after the UXB had been made safe, Thomas got bored having to do without his belongings and moved his family back home, which was a most fortunate decision as that night their hotel sustained a direct hit. Their own house was later pulled down and grandfather Thomas bought Camden Ridge from Captain Clout in the late 1950s, moving in with his wife and son, John, who later married Thelma. The wedding reception was held at Camden Ridge.

Thelma and John have three children, Martyn, Muriel and Valerie. The youngest, Valerie, is an authority on restoring gilt furniture and has been commissioned to work in such fascinating places as Fishmonger's Hall and the Mansion House. Muriel later married Paul and they have two children, Emma and Charles, who love to explore the garden and old stable block when they visit. The house is flanked by trees, but if the steeply banked garden steps are climbed to the top a wonderful view can be seen across the area. Hidden among the ferns along the sandy banks are foxholes, and the family are used to seeing foxes trotting purposefully along their garden paths.

Camden Ridge nestles among sheltering trees. The house is seen here from the top of the garden which is reached by winding stone steps. There is an outstanding view across the valley.

John and Thelma Jenkins in the garden of Camden Ridge for their wedding reception in 1952.

A feature of the sitting room which often puzzles visitors is the hearth apparently without a chimney. The fireplace is still sometimes used for open fires and the smoke is directed through a concealed chimney at the side of the window.

Grandfather Thomas, his wife Rose and son John Jenkins in the garden near to where the foxes have made their home in the bank.

Each beautifully inlaid panel in this room is different.

The entrance hall of Camden Ridge with carved choir stall seats and unusual black staircase.

Thirteen

Coopers

There was a house on the site of the present Coopers on Hawkwood Lane in the early seventeenth century, but this largely made way for a grander structure built in the eighteenth century for Francis Cooper. The next owner was a High Court Judge, Sir Richard Adams, who is buried in the grounds of St Nicholas Church having apparently succumbed to a bout of gaol fever in 1774. Captain Henry Bowden owned the house in the nineteenth century and donated a parcel of land opposite his main gates for the building of St Mary's Catholic Church. The house continued in private ownership until 1908 when the estate was purchased for use as a private boarding school for girls and became known as Tudor Hall School. The school remained here until the beginning of the Second World War when it was moved to Oxfordshire.

In 1945, the estate was acquired by Kent County Council and in 1949 became the Chislehurst site of Chislehurst and Sidcup County Technical School for Girls. New buildings were erected in the grounds in the 1960s and the Sidcup site was closed. The school was known as Coopers and later became co-educational.

Coopers School has expanded, building new study centres in the spacious grounds, but the original elegant mansion is kept as the school's Sixth Form Centre and Centre for Business Studies.

At the top of Hawkwood Lane near Coopers is the old fire station, built in the late nineteenth century to deal with the many fires which broke out on the Common. It is now HQ for the Commons Conservators who protect the use of the common lands. An old wooden clapboard house still standing was built at the start of the eighteenth century and did service as Chislehurst's first police station.

Tudor House School for Girls when at Coopers, early 1940s. The square central building with its classical portico is the original old house. Formerly, there were a group of fine cedars on the lawn. Now only one remains.

Coopers from the air. As was often the custom with large houses, the front of the house faces the lawns and was reached by a carriage drive (in this case leading from Hawkwood Lane) running parallel with the back of the house. Hawkwood house, rebuilt in 1960, can be seen across the road.

Coopers' Cedar tree weighed down by snow in the 1960s.

Greek barefoot dancing beside the rhododendrons was a popular summer activity. 'Heads up and shoulders back' children used to be taught for good posture.

Tudor Hall, Chislehurst, — Tennis Courts.

With extensive grounds there was plenty of room for tennis, a muscle-developing activity given the weighty racquets of the day.

Two views of the grounds of Tudor Hall School.

Tudor Hall, Chislehurst. — In the Grounds

Tudor Hall School's Prep Room where girls worked under supervision preparing for the following day's school work...the boarders' equivalent of homework.

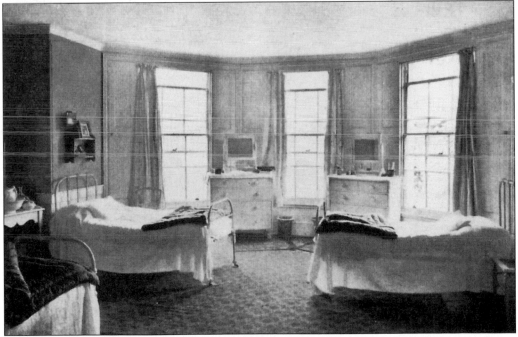

This dormitory is quite luxurious considering that many bedrooms of ordinary houses had only linoleum or polished rugs on their floors at the time. Beside each window are shutters to secure the windows at night and in bad weather. Open windows meant plenty of fresh air and healthy pupils!

Terry Moyle explained that the ornate ceiling in the dining room is still in immaculate state, thanks to Coopers' School authorities taking casts of the pattern to enable it to be reproduced exactly, whenever needed.

Near the tennis courts at Coopers.

Fourteen

Camden Place and the Imperial Family

William Camden, historian, came to Chislehurst in 1609 to escape the London plague and completed his The Annals of Queen Elizabeth here. He wished to be buried at St Nicholas' church but society deemed it more fitting he be buried at Westminster Abbey, where his memorial rests in Poet's Corner. Camden Place was named after him in 1760 by George Pratt, later Lord Chief Justice. Pratt expanded the house, gradually increasing the 2 acre estate to take in a considerable portion of the Common to about 225 acres. He intended to enclose part of St. Nicholas' land but the incumbent called a halt. He died in 1794. His son and successor, John Pratt, went to Ireland as Lord Lieutenant. In 1805 the house was sold to a prosperous merchant, Thomson Bonar and his wife Anne who already owned the adjoining 600 acre Elmstead estate. Thomson's ambitions were curtailed on the morning of 31 May 1813 when their footman of two weeks, Philip Nicholson, late of the Dragoons, murdered the two 70yr olds in their beds for no discernable reason. He attempted suicide but was saved to stand trial, where he was sentenced 'to be drawn on a hurdle to the place of execution, then to be hanged, and afterwards his body to be dissected and anatomised', a harsh sentence indeed.

Chislehurst blossomed with the arrival of newly exiled Napoleon III and Empress Eugenie. Their lifestyle demanded many servants, some of whom came from the village, others from France (who mainly lived around Mill Place). The emperor quickly entered into the social scene, receiving royalty and nobility at Camden Place, rented from Nathaniel Strode. One local tradesperson pleased to converse with the often lonely Emperor on his daily constitutional across the Common was George Cooling who, having been a butler, was not daunted by the aristocracy. For social occasions requiring additional staff, George buttled at Camden Place as well as other large Chislehurst houses. The Emperor and Empress's only child, Louis, Prince Imperial, was born in Paris. He was privately tutored before joining Royal Woolwich Military Academy as an officer cadet in 1872, coming 7th in his year. In January 1873 the Emperor, who had been ill for some time, died before Louis could be brought to him from Woolwich. The elaborate funeral cortege stretched from Camden place across the Common to St. Nicholas Church. Some years later an even more lavish funeral was held for the Prince Imperial across the same route.

In 1894 the house was established as Camden Place Limited, the headquarters of Chislehurst Golf Club, who are still in residence.

Camden Place seen through the trees of the surrounding woods.

The porphyry fireplace in the billiard room, Camden Place, was a gift to Empress Eugenie by Ferdinand de Lessops when she attended the Suez Canal opening. Above it is a picture of the Prince of Imperial. Hanging on a nearby rack are several old metal billiard cue cases, some initialled and with their own padlocks.

Lord Camden, after whom the house is named.

Mr Monk grieved when incendiary bombs hit the original dining room, badly damaging it. He and his family often dined there before the fire. 'The tapestries on the walls (were) smoke-damaged, a part of history gone forever.' Panelling was transported from a hunting lodge in France to line Lord Camden's dining room, specifically built in the same proportions so the panels could be fitted. The unusual locks on the carved doors are also French.

The Prince's monument erected by Empress Eugenie opposite Camden Place.

A richly coloured blue settle from the French Imperial occupancy of the house is now in the Billiard Room.

Camden Place from the golf course.

On the golf course is a facsimile of Lysicrates' 'Lanthorn of Demosthenes' Athenic monument. It incorporated six Corinthian columns surmounted by a floral vase. In 1954 the Lanthorn was refurbished and the columns covered over. A Club silver trophy was made in the original image.

Mrs Clara Lamb's father helped rescue the body of the Prince Imperial from the Zulus. Mrs Lamb, now in her seventies, is an expert on English heraldic embroidery on which she co-authored a book. *The Beckenham Advertiser* described Mrs Lamb laying flowers at the Prince Imperial's monument on the anniversary of his death.

Derek Lamb's grandfather, Thomas Lloyd, aged 24, was a trooper in the seventeenth Lancers, part of the contingent sent to retrieve the body of the Prince Imperial after the Zulu attack. On June 12 1879 Thomas sent a letter to his family in Beckenham from Landsmans Drift describing the troops' arrival at Rorke's Drift where the 24th Regiment were massacred. He wrote: '[I] saw a sight [I] never wanted to see again...we buried some, and came away, saw no Zulus, burnt their kraals...there were wagons and provisions lying about in all directions; we brought 35 wagons away...On marching into one place, we heard a rumour that the Prince Imperial had been killed with three others. We, the men, did not take much notice of it, as we often hear all sorts of yarns, but the next morning we found it was true. The Prince was lying in a lagger with two others. I saw them, they were all naked and disembowelled. We took the Prince back to camp.' The letter is proudly kept by Mrs Clara Lamb, Thomas Lloyd's daughter.

THE LATE PRINCE IMPERIAL—THE ATTACK.

The Imperial family: Emperor Napoleon III, Empress Eugenie and the Prince Imperial at the moment of his attack by Zulus. As an observer, Louis left for Cape Town. He, Capt. Carey, six of Major Beddington's men and a native tracker went to the Umbazani River on recconnaisance. Stopping for coffee, they turned their horses loose in tall grass. Their tracker sighted Zulus, gave a warning shout and the detachment leaped to their horses as 40 rifles fired on them. The Prince's horse, frightened by the noise, broke away and Louis was left alone to run after his party, riding for their lives; nineteen Zulus assegais hit him as he fell. The next day his body was found and borne back to Chislehurst in state.

ROYAL MILITARY ACADEMY, WOOLWICH.
TASMA PHOTO.

Woolwich Royal Military Academy where The Prince Imperial attended military school.

The Royal Artillery and other regiments on parade outside the Garrison Church of the Academy on Woolwich Common at the end of the nineteenth century.

Fifteen

Social Scenes and Cinema

Even before the advent of the Imperial Family, Chislehurst had its share of social life. The seventeenth century well-to-do moved from London to avoid the plagues and Chislehurst suited nicely, being less than an hour's ride by horse, coach or carriage from the capital. Frognal, Camden, Foxbury (where Pat Bushell's mother was a housemaid and often recalled the lavish parties held there) and numerous large houses in the area held balls, soirees, supper parties and formal dinners, inviting local gentry and friends from the City. When the Empress and retinue left the village and the estates were sold off, the social scene mainly revolved around Chislehurst's Clubs and Societies. The Cricket Club, formerly West Kent for the gentlemen and Chislehurst for the players, now amalgamated. Their grounds, opposite William Willetts house, are next to Camden Place where their annual ball is the social event of the year. The club has the legal right to their grounds on the understanding that it is kept in good condition. Douglas Wright, England's best leg-break bowler, was a member and played for Kent before and after the war. He lived with his parents in Park Road and his father owned a popular lemonade shop in the village. Colin Cowdray, England player, married Penny Cheesemen, daughter of the Cricket Club chairman, Stuart Cheeseman, at St Nicholas' Church and Peter May was his best man. Unfortunately the wedding coincided with Biggin Hill's 1956 Air Show and the choir boys, who preferred Air displays to anthems, refused to sing until they each received autographs from the whole England team who were attending the wedding.

In these days when churches are frequently deconsecrated and used for other purposes, Chislehurst broke the mould by turning their cinema into a church. The original tip-up seats were retained and the congregation sit in luxury while attending Mass at St Patrick's Catholic Church in the High Street. When it was still a cinema, films were reported in local newspapers and scenes from the film were displayed outside the cinema during its run there.

As well as Chislehurst's Poultry Society, Gardener's Mutual Improvement Society, Football and Rugby clubs, there were the Guides, Scouts and local Drama in the form of The Imperial Players at the Methodist Church, as well as many other clubs, some of which still flourish.

Steve 'Jonty' Hart remembers Smokey Joe who travelled the area in the 1950s when in his late sixties, pushing an old, tyre-less byke with a perpetually smoking Primus stove on his back. He was regularly in and out of Queen Mary's Hospital for various ailments. Smokey's friend was Mr Long who had a wooden leg.

The Kent Hounds, Chelsfield, in 1936, hasn't changed much. A popular halt for ramblers, publican Jean Crossfield believes it was originally a draper's shop selling ale as a side line. It is on a country track, once the main road running to the Rock and Fountain, and the present B-road did not exist.

Chislehurst and environs are well provided with congenial social venues, including public houses such as The Tiger's Head, The Sydney Arms, The Bull, Rambler's Rest, Fox and Hounds, The Crown and The Queen's Head, most of which were originally eighteenth-century hostelries. Wandering Smokey Joe, a local character, pushed his bicycle and all his personal possessions on regular tours around from Chislehurst through Sidcup and frequently stopped at The Sydney Arms for a meal or free drink.

Bishop's Well, formerly Old Crown Cottage, then Mayricks. Mr and Mrs Wollaston held a reception for the late Prince Imperial. Mrs F. Draper recalls a doodlebug landing in front of the house which was re-built after the war. Mr Gressier, the dentist, his wife and daughter Sue lived here until they returned to Australia. The house is now owned by Mr and Mrs Ramsay. Head Prefect Alison Wilson, centre, front row, with all the Chislehurst and Sidcup Technical School Prefects in the school cloisters, 1949/50 when Barbara (Monk) Waine attended.

It was always fun being a Girl Guide at camp and these lucky local girls are enjoying a week under canvas.

Patrol leader Doris Keane with the smart tent and her patrol.

Chislehurst caves are a vast, ancient network of chalk-hewn passages extending many miles under the area. During the war they sheltered several thousand people from as far away as London. Rose Gravener remembers her Dad paying 6d each a week to sleep there; children went free. Volunteers made 'huge piles of bread and butter and dripping. It was well organised. Children had tea, then straight to bed...Falling bombs weren't heard in the caves...People took their best eiderdowns and slept in numbered bunks with notches cut into the chalk for candles. On the wireless Lord Haw-Haw threatened "We haven't forgotten the people in Chislehurst Caves."' There was a pervasive damp smell and clothes easily rotted if kept there long. People got on with their lives during the day then slept overnight in the caves with a few creature comforts. Ablution facilities, central cooking and other necessities were provided. Dances and other social events held underground were well attended. Regular Church services were held at the caves' own altar and all manner of meetings were held in the caverns: discos are still popularly held there. Rose recalls there were separate toilets for men and women: 'you walked in one end and out the other. Only one night this man got in the wrong one and there were all these women with their long knickers down around their ankles - you should have heard them scream!' Graham Sugden says that because there was fear that a bombing raid could trap people by causing the soft chalk entrance to collapse, an alternative escape route was provided via a long, cylindrical metal pipe which was uncomfortably negotiated on hands and knees.

When the Scadbury and Frognal estates were sold in 1915 the sale included Rose Cottage Laundry near The Sidney Arms. The tenant paid £148. 6s. 6d. rental per annum. In 1915 this was sold together with Battle's Baker's shop on Royal Parade, (rent £75 p.a.) opposite The Bull, as Lots 35 and 77. Frogpool Farm, now the Equestrian Centre, was Lot 21, rental £100 p.a. Mr and Mrs Lloyd keep a copy of the original catalogue, in which their own house features.

Now turned into modern flats, St Michael's Orphanage was once both a workhouse and (in 1861) home for the area's destitute children.

It was a case of all hands on deck: everyone who had a car or other vehicle was expected to be there at Chislehurst station when the Belgians and British wounded arrived from the trenches. Some sent their cars with chauffeurs; some drove there themselves, but they all responded.

The wedding of Old Farrington's pupil G. Meglaughlin on 20 April 1922.

Pupils of Burnt Oak Lane School passing what were the school's old cottages, opposite, at Lamorbey, Sidcup. The school was built in 1840 and the smaller cottages in 1841.